Turning
Ornaments
&
Eggs

Dick Sing

Schiffer Publishing Ltd

4880 Lower Valley Road, Atglen, PA 19310 USA

Gallery set-up and cover styling by Cindy Sing

Copyright © 2002 by Dick Sing
Library of Congress Control Number: 2001099447

Designed by Bonnie M. Hensley
Cover design by Bruce M. Waters
Type set in Korinna BT

ISBN: 0-7643-1463-7
Printed in China

Published by Schiffer Publishing Ltd.
4880 Lower Valley Road
Atglen, PA 19310
Phone: (610) 593-1777; Fax: (610) 593-2002
E-mail: Schifferbk@aol.com
Please visit our web site catalog at **www.schifferbooks.com**
We are always looking for people to write books on new and related subjects. If you have an idea for a book, please contact us at the above address.

This book may be purchased from the publisher.
Include $3.95 for shipping.
Please try your bookstore first.
You may write for a free catalog.

In Europe, Schiffer books are distributed by
Bushwood Books
6 Marksbury Avenue
Kew Gardens
Surrey TW9 4JF England
Phone: 44 (0) 20 8392 8585
Fax: 44 (0) 20 8392 9876
E-mail: Bushwd@aol.com
Free postage in the UK. Europe: air mail at cost.

Dedications

Cindy,

who helps me choose the proper words, does my typing,
withstands my frustrations, and helps with my inspiration.
My life would be lacking without my soul mate and best friend.

I take this liberty, as well I might
To dedicate this book, that I helped write

Tis to a man, by name Dick Sing
I know him well, I wear his ring

With a skew, chisel and gouge
He will please the crowd

From bowls to pens and captive rings
He has no secrets, he shares these things

He travels through the United States, and even Down Under
His demos are popular, he is quite a wonder

I'll end this now with just one thing
I am proud of this man, by name Dick Sing

Cindy

Contents

Introduction

This book has been written to offer woodturning projects that are a little more challenging. I consider these projects very satisfying. The ornaments challenge me more in the sense that they have to have a more delicate look, style, and feel. No matter how many I make, I always seem to come across a different combination of woods that I feel can make the ornament even better. I always feel the globe could be thinner or lighter, or the thinness and delicateness of the spindle could be tweaked. I look back at some of my first ornaments, which I thought were spectacular, and am disappointed in them.

I have improved over the years and hope to continue improving in the future. My first spindle (or icicle) was angular without any flow to it. Similarly, I did not start with a captive ring on the ornaments—now it is a signature of sorts. It is the little nuances that make or break the piece.

When it comes to turning eggs, we take them for granted. The egg is probably nature's most perfect form. Even in a pan sunny side up they look good. Getting the form correct on an egg, however, rivals the most difficult form in turning: it is difficult to make an egg look like an egg. The entire egg is an ever changing curve and very susceptible to flat spots or angular planes. I prefer my eggs to look like Mother Nature smiled on them.

There are people who have egg collections made of various woods, and this includes my wife and me. The wooden egg goes back to a time when women used them to darn socks. I remember my mother using one when I was a child. (I think it may have been a dinosaur egg.)

I guess the day I feel my work could not be improved upon is the day they will nail the lid shut, as it would mean I have quit learning. As good as one piece may seem, there is always room for improvement, change, and learning.

One thing that I ask is please read the book. The pictures are nice and hopefully do tell a story, but there are a thousand words between them that create the whole picture.

Ornaments

An ornament—with its gently rounded globe of figured wood hollowed out to a thin walled lightness and its contrasting, delicately tapered finial—always seems to inspire awe in people. Many people are afraid to tackle a project of this magnitude. I usually hear, "I can't do that. How do you hollow out something you can't see? How do you make a finial that thin without breaking it? I wish I could do it." I tell them they *can* do it. All it takes is an understanding of the hollowing out process along with the setting up of the delicate spindle. From this point on, it is all a matter of learning how to handle the tools, understanding their function, and knowing how they work in coordination with your hands and body movements.

To start off our globe, I have a scrap block in the four jaw chuck that has been faced off and flat. This could also be attached to a face plate or screw chuck. The block of wood I'm going to use for the globe is ambrosia maple. The type of wood selected should have nice figure or natural character that really stands out. Another criterion would be the weight of the wood itself: a piece of ambrosia maple, for example, is relatively light, as opposed to desert ironwood, which is very dense and heavy. We would have to make the desert ironwood extremely thin to make it light. I use a piece approximately 2" square or whatever your stock or design lends itself to. Find and mark the center of the end you will consider to be the bottom of the globe.

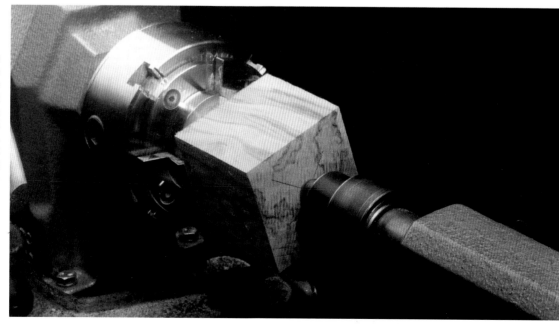

Make a dry run by putting the work block between the scrap block and the live center. Make sure everything goes together—we will use this setup to center the wood to the scrap block when gluing it on as we will not have time to dally. Turn back your tailstock and remove your work block.

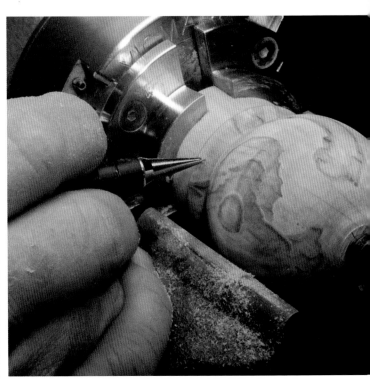

Cover the ways of your lathe with a paper towel. If you drip glue, it may as well be on something other than the metal surfaces. Now apply medium density cyanoacrylate glue to the block, hit the scrap block with the accelerator, fit the block to the live center, and crank it into the scrap block. Immediately rotate the chuck and the work piece block in opposite directions by hand to spread the glue. If you have dallied, forgo the last sentence as time and Super Glue™ wait for no man.

Refine the shape on the bottom, or tailstock end, but do not progress too far on the top as we need all the strength we can for the hollowing out process. Look at your existing shape and, in your mind's eye, estimate where the top of the globe's final shape will fall when finished. We will be working the first half initially, before the back or top half.

Using a 3/8" spindle gouge, rough out the basic shape of your globe.

Check your work piece to see if it has any imperfections that need to be addressed. Ambrosia maple is notorious for having cracks in the spalt areas. Many times you cannot see these until the piece has been sanded and there is dust in the cracks. As a precaution, we will try and get a jump on the situation.

Using a piece of polyethylene packing material, spread water thin cyanoacrylate over the entire surface and hit with accelerator. This will stabilize cracks and soft spots. This step is not necessary with all woods. If used, however, it should be done when your shape is just about complete (except for the area by the scrap block). It is not a cure-all, but can help at times.

Continue until the surface is ready to be sanded.

Using a shear cut, lightly clean up the surface.

The most difficult area to hollow is the very center at the axis, as it is rotating the slowest. We are going to kill the proverbial two birds with one stone. By drilling down the center, we will eliminate that portion plus establish a known diameter at the top of the globe. This will be necessary when we cut if off and make the top finial for the globe. I am using a 3/8" drill, but whatever suits your design is what you should use. I have yet to find a wood lathe that did not have a small amount of play in the tailstock. If the tailstock was locked down in its most out of line position, we would drill an oversized hole. I prefer to leave the tailstock loose and advance the drill point lightly against the rotating work piece, which will allow the tailstock to seek its center. At this point, lock down the tailstock. Now continue to drill completely through the work piece. If you are going to use a shop vacuum to remove the shavings, as I do, drill completely through the scrap block. This will give an air access hole for air to enter through the scrap block. Otherwise you will create a vacuum block, making it difficult to remove the shavings. The alternative is to remove the entire chuck from the lathe and shake the shavings out. As obvious as this may seem, do not remove the work piece from the chuck. Remove the entire chuck and work piece as a unit.

Using a 1/4" square round nose scraper, start to clean out the inside. I am opening up the hole in the bottom slightly to gain additional access room. My finished hole will be 5/8" and I want to stay under that dimension right now as the tools will probably come in contact with it during the hollowing. Position your tool rest where the cutting edge of your scraper is at center line or slightly below. The speed I am running is approximately 1200 rpm.

To achieve cutting around a corner, therefore, we need a curved tool. The tool that I am showing here is very high tech—it's called an Allen wrench. I have ground it so that it has flats on the bottom (to be stable on the tool rest) and top (to provide for a cutting edge). I have used the curve of the wrench as my cutting edge, it having been ground with a scraper angle. Do not leave too much of an offset as the torque from cutting will then have a tendency to twist the tool in your hand. It may not be the best steel, but it will definitely serve its purpose (as I have hollowed out many with it) — and the price is right. This tool is again used at center line or slightly below. As far as the removing of the inside material, it is a matter of feel along with smooth, controlled motions.

Using a straight scraper through a small opening on a globe type object presents a problem. Trying to get around a corner, near the bottom the tool fouls out on the edge of the opening, preventing us from attaining our goal.

As we continue our ornament, you may notice a different pattern or figure in the globe. This is due to an "aw shit" moment, illustrated here. The cause was a crack that developed but I didn't notice it until after I had heard it—which was too late. Now that you know I am mortal, you won't have to feel like the Lone Ranger if it happens to you as well.

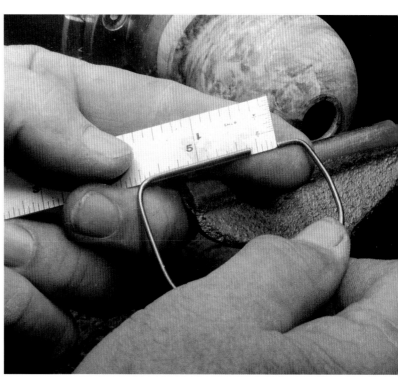

You know that old adage about changing horses in the middle of the stream? Well we've done it. Due to our design alteration, we now have replaced the broken globe with a different block and have progressed to the same stage where we left off, sans the erose opening. The globe is now maple burl (looks better anyway!). Next we need to start measuring what we have for a wall thickness.

As you can see, the gap between the two pieces of wire is 5/16" and shaped in such a position that it will go inside the globe.

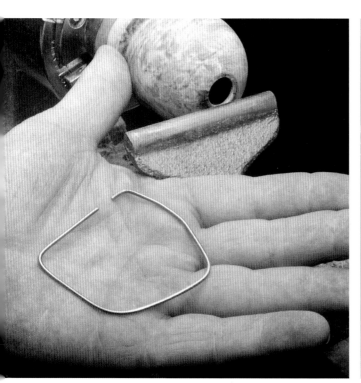

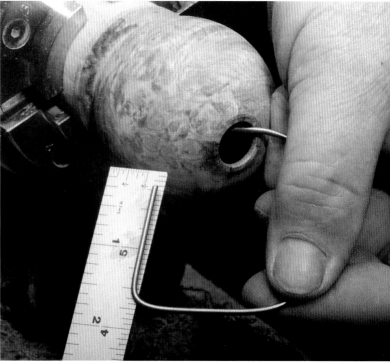

Another high tech tool. It's called a piece of coat hanger. I chose coat hanger wire because it has a certain amount of memory—in other words, you can lightly spring it and it will return to its original shape. If you used mild steel wire, it would not return to its original shape. We're not talking about being heavy handed with the springing, just within reason. Music wire will work too, but it is more difficult to form.

With one leg of the gauge contacting the inside surface of the globe and the gap between the outside of the globe and the other leg of the gauge being 1/4", this leaves a wall thickness of 1/16". The desired wall thickness is determined by your nerve and cutting ability. Once the ornament is put together, wall thickness will not be visible unless there is a natural void or intentional holes are added. The only indication will be the ornament's weight . . . or weightless-ness.

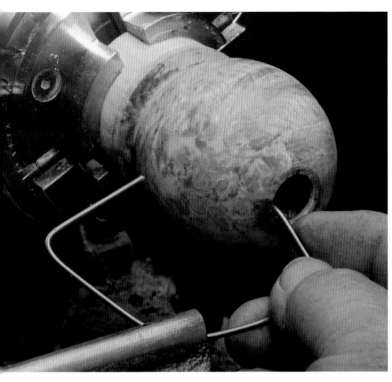

I have worked the inside to its finished dimension on approximately half the globe. I did not work the other half as I needed the strength to hold the piece while turning. If we had worked the half that is glued to the scrap block first, we would have no strength to work the opposite end.

As discussed during the initial shaping of the globe, we had to use our mind's eye to determine where the top of the globe would ultimately be. We now need to take a critical measurement. I simply use my finger as a depth stop on the tool, with the cutting edge placed where I estimate the inside top of the globe will be.

Hollow out part of the top half with the 1/4" round nose scraper, being sure to leave material for the finished shape. Now that we have the bulk of the inside material removed, we can start shaping the top of the globe. Do not cut away too much as we still need the extra support.

This picture shows the estimated amount of material needed to be removed from the inside top of the globe. This is not the Bible, but a general "guesstimate" taken strictly by eye.

If you notice, the gauge has been reversed in this picture. In the original position—short leg inside—I could not measure the top. With a little preplanning when making your gauge, you can reverse it and use the long leg on the inside and the short leg on the outside to reach the top, relatively square to the surface of the globe, which will give a reasonably accurate measurement.

Continuing to shape the top of the globe. You may have to work both the inside and outside in unison to maintain both the form and wall thickness. Remember, we have a 3/8" diameter hole through the center.

I am cutting away some of the scrap block to give myself room to work the top end of the globe. Again, this is the versatility of scrap blocks. By using scrap wood, we increase the holding area, which saves expensive wood or provides a means of attaching small pieces and yet allows room for cutting away for tool clearance.

I have completed forming the top of the globe and am now ready to sand. I do not attempt to make a perfectly round globe, as I believe the little nuances of shape are what make each globe unique. I *have* made near perfect globes, but I prefer those that are *not* perfect.

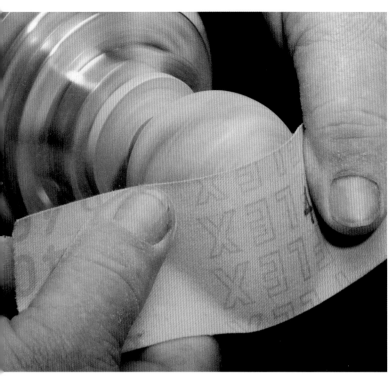

Sanding the globe is next. Start with the appropriate grit for the surface. Work out all imperfections before moving on to the next grit. The next grit will not remove the imperfections, but will enhance them, or make them stand out. I usually sand to 400 grit.

I am using Deft™ to finish my globe. Apply a liberal coat, allow to set for a couple of minutes, and wipe off the excess with a paper towel. Then cover with a paper towel to protect your glasses and whatever else, turn on the lathe, and lightly buff. This works similarly to a French polish. You may want to use more than one coat, according to your preferences. No matter how many coats of finish you put on, the final result will be dictated by how well you have prepared the surface.

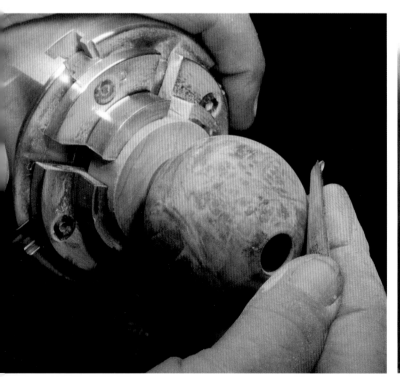

When you have finished sanding, stop the lathe and hand sand. This will help to remove any concentric sanding marks, which are always left when sanding with the lathe running.

Using a 5/8" Fostner bit, drill the bottom hole to your finished dimension. At this point, the globe is very thin and held on by a minimal amount of wood. Use care when drilling, as vibrations are a factor and can cause problems.

I am cutting a flat where the icicle part of the ornament will attach. Use caution when cutting this, as you have nothing much holding the globe and you're a long way from the attached surface. Vibrations or worse can happen easily. The reason this is being cut after finishing is that it will make a good clean glue surface.

I am using a parting tool to cut the globe free from the remainder of the block. As you cut this, try to establish a size of the flat that will correspond to the finial, which we will make later. Also, cut with a slight concave as you did on the bottom.

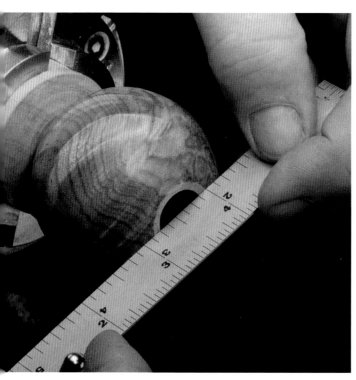

Make this slightly concave so only the very edges contact, which will make for a nice tight joint.

The best laid plans of mice and men often go awry. If, after cutting the globe free, you have found something you dislike (such as a mismatch at the top or poor sanding), it is not impossible to fix. Using the scrap remaining on my chuck, I have made a small tenon to hold and drive the globe from the bottom or 5/8" hole.

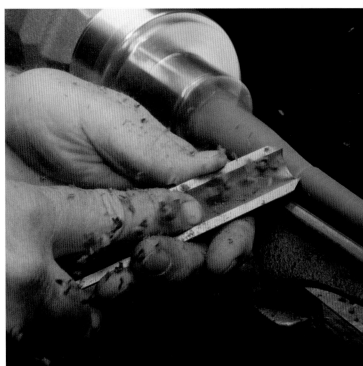

By using the tenon to hold and drive the globe, and with the tailstock's live center in the opposing hole, we now have a situation similar to spindle turning and can lightly adjust any imperfections. The bottom of the globe should be to your expectations as it was in the open all the time. The top is normally where lack of room caused error.

Using a roughing gouge, I am reducing the blank to a cylinder in preparation for layout.

Now that we have the globe completed, it's time for the icicle. When choosing your wood, try to get a relatively straight grain piece. Also, I prefer a contrasting color. The size is strictly determined by your design. Mine happens to be moradillo, 1" square by about 8-1/2" long. This provides enough wood for both the icicle and the top finial on my design. I hold the blank in a four jaw chuck with long jaws. These happen to be a set I had made up, but any jaws that will hold the work piece will be fine. We also need a live center in the tailstock, preferably with a cone center. This combination allows for the chuck to hold and drive the work piece without end pressure from the tailstock. The tailstock's only purpose will be to support the end of the spindle. In fact, the pressure is so light that if you touched the live center it would stop rotating. If we tried to do this between centers, we would have to have enough pressure on the tailstock to drive the work piece, which would probably put a bow in the icicle as it is reduced down in size, giving us vibration and turning problems. This is not a solve-all setup, but it sure helps.

Using a skew, I am reducing my stock thickness even more.

The icicle to this point.

Using the tip of the skew, mark out the features of the icicle.

One day, as I was turning ornaments, I had several laying on my work bench. Out of all those ornaments, one stood out from the rest. I took that ornament and made a story stick for its icicle. By doing this, I can now use it to establish my proportions any time. I don't worry about the diameters as my eye determines them in relationship to the whole icicle. If every one were exactly the same, they would look too mechanical to me. Another advantage of the story stick is that if you lose your marks while reducing the diameter you can recreate them easily.

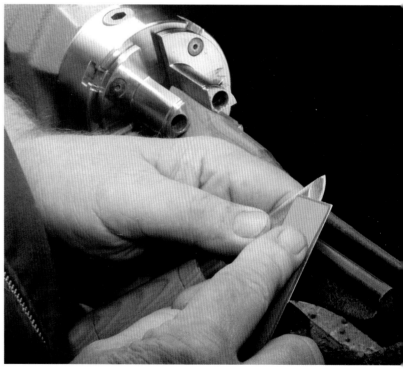

Remember that you want your tools to be sharp. The skew is normally the only tool that I sharpen with a diamond hone. It only takes a second to touch it up. I found the small skew I am using here on a bargain table. For this delicate work, it seems to work nicely for me, although I have made a lot of spindles using a normal 1/2" skew. Again, being mortal, I am a tool junkie.

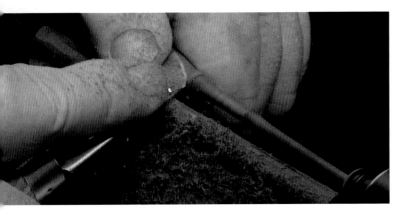

I am starting to form the steps of the icicle. The lathe speed is as fast as it will go because of the very small diameter. We are really not concerned with rpm, more with surface speed (although rpm governs it), which affects the cutting action. The surface distance traveled by the small diameter of the icicle in one revolution is nowhere near the distance traveled by a 12" bowl. Needless to say, we would have to slow down with a larger diameter. Find a speed where the wood cuts cleanly. If you are going to err on a wood lathe, be safe and err with a slower speed.

Using a 1/4" spindle gouge, I am creating my design by adding some embellishment.

Continuing up the icicle, forming the designs. Be sure to work from your tailstock, or thinner end, back—towards the headstock. Notice that I am supporting the work piece with my fingers. I'm applying the same pressure with my supporting hand as I am with the tool. If I were pressing too hard with the tool, you would see a wisp of smoke curl off my fingers and they would be medium well done in no time, so this is a light control situation. It is also very important to keep your tool in a cutting position versus a scraping position. In a scraping position, with the cutting edge being at the center line, the work piece would have a tendency to climb the cutting edge and shatter. Another problem encountered with very thin spindles involves the starting and stopping of the lathe. If your lathe is not equipped with a slow start drive and starts out at the motor's given rpm, the inertia against the thin spindle trying to start the live center will have a tendency to snap the spindle. This is another reason to position your live center without much pressure. Another help is to take your hand on the handwheel and give it a spin as you turn on the lathe. As obvious as this may sound, if you are using this assist, make sure you start the rotation in the proper direction. If you don't, you will compound the situation.

Continuing to work out our design.

One of the trademarks I have developed for my ornaments is a captive ring. A captive ring is a ring formed and cut free between two larger diameters, which totally traps it. At this point, we want to start taking this into consideration. If the material for the ring is eliminated, there will be nothing to construct it with.

Cleaning off the glue and finalizing the shape of our ring.

Starting to form our ring.

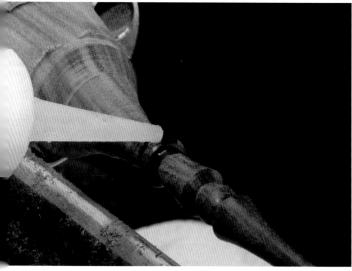

When making a captive ring this small, some of the pores in the grain are larger than cracks. To help ourselves here, flood the ring with water thin cyanoacrylate. I like to protect my tools and lathe with a shop towel or paper towel below.

For these small captive rings, I have made a tool from a dental pick (found at a flea market) to get under the ring and cut it free. Being this small, it is not really a good cutting tool, as I have made it ambidextrous to cut left or right. Given the tool's poor cutting edge — basically just a sharp point — the technique involves basically whittling away the material, working from both sides.

Starting to relieve the underside of the ring. I normally have a very good light source so I can see exactly what I'm doing. Due to the incompatibility of incandescent light with the photography for this book, however, I'm working without the strong light I normally use. Make sure you have sufficient light for your work.

Continue cutting to free the ring.

As you get your ring close to being cut free, take the time to sand. After it's cut free it will be too late—holding the loose ring while sanding at that point would become quite futile, kind of like chasing a bear with a flyswatter.

I have cut the ring loose and am now holding it aside with my finger and working out underneath it.

I'm using a light shearing cut to get the area that was beneath the ring clean.

Starting to work the area where the tenon will be that attaches to the globe. Measure the surface on the globe that has the flat where the icicle will mate. Make sure the mating surface on the icicle will match, as we want these two to be in agreement.

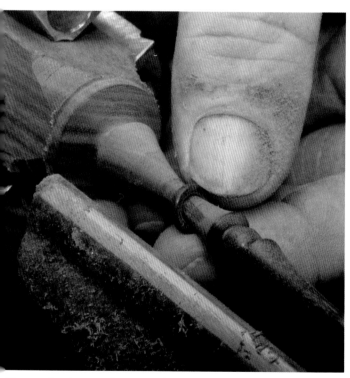

The captive ring now has enough clearance to float freely. This area is ready for sanding.

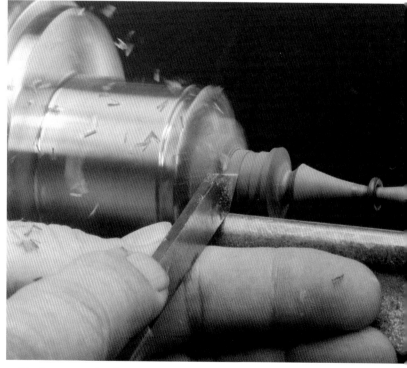

Starting to cut the diameter for the tenon. A trick I use is to cut two sizes next to each other, favoring the one that I will be using. In other words, I will be taking two measurements at a time. My actual tenon is always the larger size and I cut a smaller one next to it, on the scrap side, which will be cut off with time. If the smaller tenon is still oversize, I know I can cut my actual tenon to that dimension or slightly below, which gives me a visual reference. I then cut the second tenon smaller. If that one is too small, I know not to go that deep. This way I cut my time and effort basically in half.

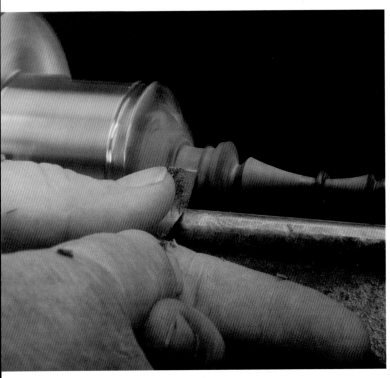

Continuing. We are just about there.

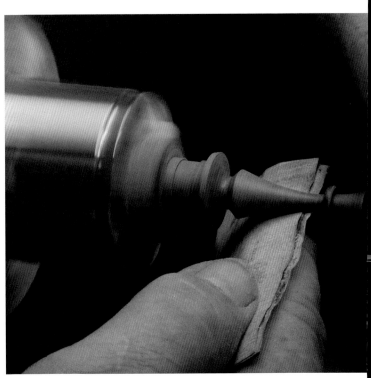

I have progressively sanded to 400 grit, using the edges of the paper to sand *to* corners, rather than over them, in an effort to keep our detail.

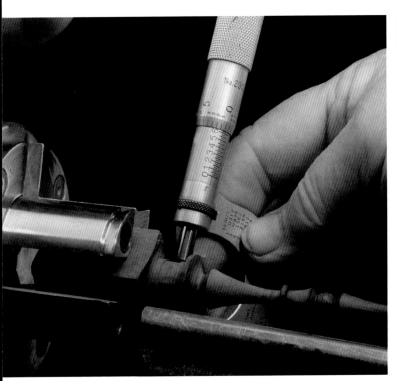

We've reached our tenon size. Undercut the surface that will be matched to the globe slightly, like we did on the mating surface, as this will insure us of that nice tight joint line. We are now ready to sand.

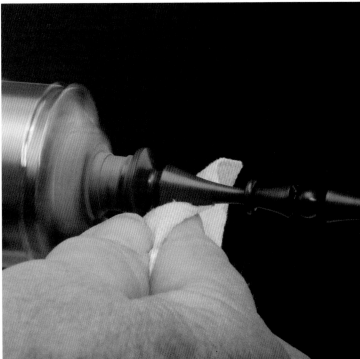

I have put on a coat of Deft™, wiped off the excess, and am now buffing the icicle. Use a paper towel for buffing, rather than a rag, as rags will not tear the way a paper towel will if it accidentally catches on a revolving part. Rags, long sleeves, gloves, and loose long hair have no place around a rotating lathe.

Using the short end or heel of the skew, roll the end of the icicle and cut it off. Sand the end and give the very end a touch of finish.

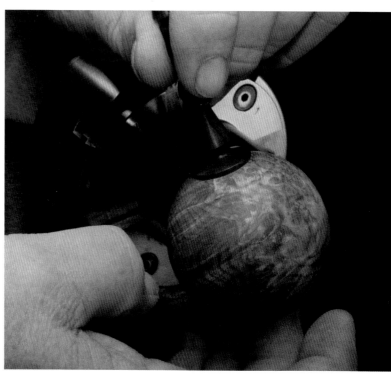

If you've done it right, you have a good joint line, or match, between the globe and the icicle.

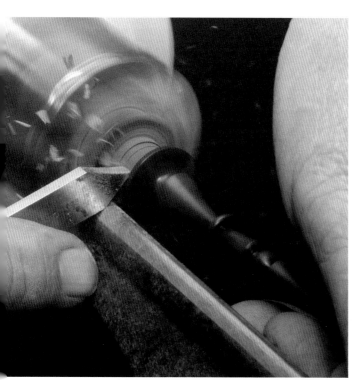

Using a parting tool, part it off.

I have now pulled the remaining stock out of the chuck far enough to make the finial.

Remove eyelet and continue shaping the finial.

Place the point of the drill against the revolving center of the work piece. Align the length of the tool to the ways. If the point of the drill has centered itself it will be very stable, as it will have found its center. If it is off center, it will dance around. If you have problems finding the center, take the tip of a skew, make a small mark at the center, and try again.

We need to put an eyelet into the finial so that we can hang the ornament. I have found that an easy way to drill the pilot hole for the eyelet is with a small, hand held chuck.

Screw in the eyelet and check to see if the ball has cracked. The reason for doing this now is that oftentimes with hard woods and small diameters, screwing in the threaded eyelet will crack the work piece. By doing it now, if it does crack, all I have to is cut off the cracked portion, move down, and recut everything. If I had completed the finial and then cracked it, I would have wasted all my time and possibly the wood I need to make the finial (depending on how much stock I had).

Shaping the finial.

Using a parting tool, start to make the tenon for the finial. This is going to end up as 3/8" to match the hole that we drilled. Again, make the mating surface of the finial concave so that it will make good contact on the edges of the globe.

As noted with the icicle, be sure the mating surfaces on the finial and the globe will agree.

Sanding the finial is next.

Finish as normal and put in your eyelet.

Part off the finial.

When I glue the pieces of my ornament together, I like to use a little yellow glue so that if I get any on the surface, it is easily removed. Super Glue™ would ruin the finish. When the glue is dry, the final step is to buff with wax on a loose bound wheel (with care). If the fit is loose and you need a clamp, use your drill press. Stand the ornament under the quill, apply light pressure, and lock.

Basic Eggs

Children who see my wooden eggs at art shows often want to know if I make them. I tell them I have a pet wooden decoy which lays them. No yolk.

The first year that Cindy and I were married our anniversary fell on Easter Sunday. A few weeks before, she asked me for a wooden Easter egg. With me being a normal husband you can guess what happened. On Easter morning we exchanged Easter baskets but Cindy's was sadly missing a wooden egg. There was no comment made, but there was disappointment in her eyes. How could I forget!

While she was ironing a dress for church she happened to notice a wooden egg alongside of the sofa. With the shriek of a young child, she came in to thank me and I then informed her there were more. I had set up an Easter egg hunt for her. There were thirteen eggs of various woods hidden around the living room. This anniversary present did not turn into a snowball but into an avalanche. I had set a precedent and not only did Cindy want them the following years, but the list now includes my mother, mother-in-law, daughter and husband (she keeps his as it is an excuse to get more), and grandsons—plus a few for my wife's special friends and clients. Last year I made thirty-five eggs to fill her order. This year, due to a windfall of additional new woods, the spring hatch topped sixty. Being my wife, Cindy receives more than one egg in her basket and they are usually the grade A eggs. Beware.

During the course of a year, when I come across a unique or new species of wood that Cindy does not have in her collection, I throw it aside for the following spring hatch. What a wonderful way to display your cherished pieces of wood! They show face and endgrain and are natures most perfect form (next to Cindy). It has become a challenge to continually find a different species or an outstanding piece of figured wood to supplement her collection.

BC (before Cindy), I had previously made eggs that looked as though they could have crippled the hen that laid them. I am not as proud of them as I was then, but I guess you could call that the evolution of a turner. Now I would like to share some of the procedures I went through in trying to perfect my eggs.

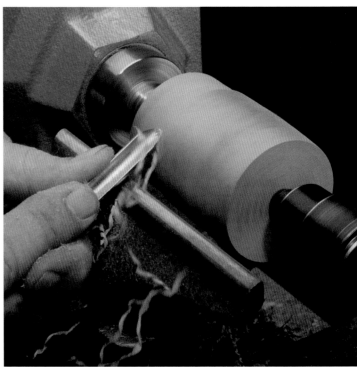

Eggs are a very difficult shape to conquer. When I look back at the first eggs I made, I consider them very unsuccessful. Some time ago, I decided I was going to make eggs that I could be more proud of. Step one was going to the refrigerator and picking out what I thought was a good egg. Step two was taking dimensions and making templates off of that egg. Very rarely do my eggs totally conform to the templates, but occasionally it is difficult to see where to change the shape. This is where the templates shine. They have also given me basic dimensions with which I can start my shape.

Reducing the square block to a cylinder.

I am starting with a block of madrone burl, approximately 2" x 2" x 3". This dimension is variable, according to whatever your stock is. The block is mounted between a cup dead center in the headstock and a rotating cup live center.

Using my template, I am laying out the dimensions. The tapered end of the egg is facing the tailstock. No reason, just habit. When laying out the egg I may reverse the blank to get around a defect. You cut away more wood on the small end.

I set a pair of calipers to my desired diameter and use the parting tool to set the same.

Eliminate the excess stock on both ends.

I have established the ends of the egg with a parting tool and reduced the diameter at the cuts to provide room to work.

Shaping the tapered end of the egg.

Beginning to shape the round end.

Progress on the shaping.

As you can see from the template, we still have a ways to go.

The egg is now close enough to the template and looks good to the eye, so we can start to finish.

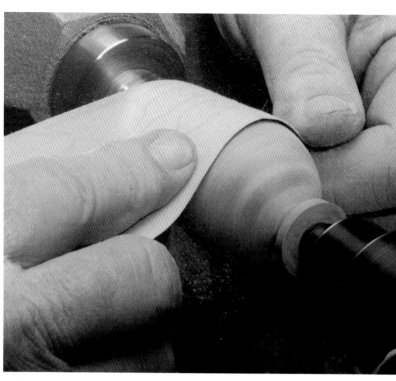

With the lathe running, lightly run your fingers over the egg. This will tell you if there are any ridges or surface defects. Your fingers will tell you things that your eyes cannot see.

Sanding the egg. Start out with a grit heavy enough to sand out the egg's imperfections.

TIP: Many times after sanding, finishing, and removing the work piece from the lathe, you will see sanding marks or imperfections in the surface that were not visible before. This is very frustrating as we either need to try and remount it or refinish by hand. When working on small pieces (or any size piece under certain conditions) it is difficult to see these sanding marks or surface imperfections due to the lighting and work angle. A simple solution is to keep a mirror handy so you can use it to reflect the light and see the surface of the piece at the proper angle before removing it from the lathe. I learned this trick as a tool and die apprentice many years ago—it was used to see around corners or when working overhead in small accesses. I have yet to see anyone else use it in woodturning.

When your sanding is complete, shut off the lathe and sand with the length by hand to eliminate concentric marks.

Liberally apply finish (I used Deft™) and let penetrate.

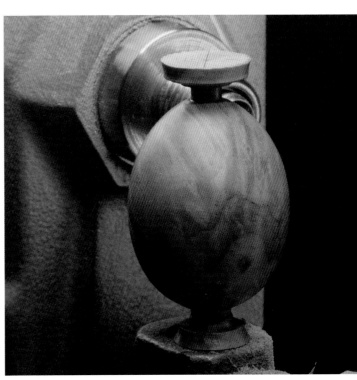

Remove the egg from between centers, but do not cut off the ends.

Wipe off the excess, turn on the lathe, and buff lightly. If you feel you need more finish, apply additional coats.

The ends of some turned eggs are my pet peeve. When shaping the ends, lack of room or excessive pressure causes the tool bevel to ride hard against the surface. Being end grain, the surface is then crushed or burnished by the bevel of the tool. This normally does not get sanded out and the end result is a non uniform finish on the ends of the egg. Another peeve of mine is that sometimes when the eggs are parted off, the end grain is torn below the surface, leaving a hole. To beat these situations, I have made a chuck that will hold the egg so I can finish both ends in the lathe.

I made my chuck to be held by a screw chuck. The only reason I used a screw chuck was that I had it. This chuck could be made for use on a face plate, to be held in a four jaw, or used with whatever means you have to adapt to. I started with a piece of hard maple approximately 3" x 3" x 3-1/2". I mounted it to my screw chuck and reduced it to a cylinder.

My second step was to drill out the center with a 1-1/2" Fostner bit approximately 1/4" deeper than the 1/2" holes.

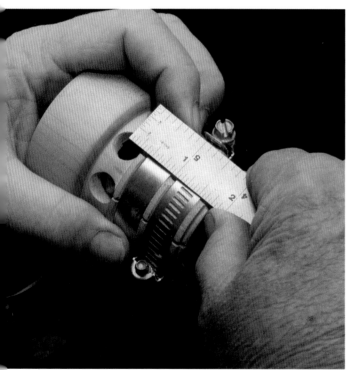

The first step was to lay out the holes that go through the cylinder using the index on my lathe. I laid out eight holes. I also marked them in a circle 1-3/4" back from what will be the face of the chuck. I made a vee-block on the table saw and positioned the center of the vee dead center under the chuck on my drill press. I then drilled 1/2" diameter holes through the chuck. If your setup is good, you can drill opposing holes at the same time. If you feel your setup is not accurate, I would only drill half way through. The purpose of these holes will be to help form the fingers, make them more flexible, and give you an access hole to help remove the egg if needed. Believe me, they are necessary.

My third step was to slightly concave the inner walls. You can see the gap between the wall and the scale, which is 90° to the bottom. This was done many years ago and I may have differed slightly in my steps, but I am doing my best to describe them for you. Another factor that plays into this is that I have made numerous chucks, some of which did not work to my liking and one of which did, but was destroyed by an errant tool rest. I also believe I contoured the inside walls to a wooden egg I had made. Whatever you do on the inside walls should be done at this stage of the game. After we cut the fingers, they will not allow you to turn inside without vibration.

33

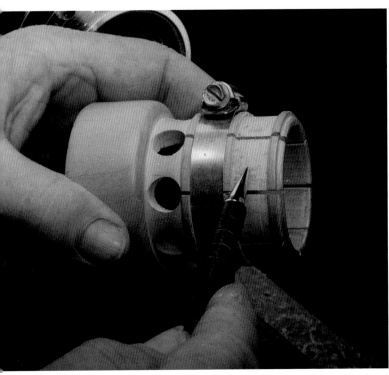

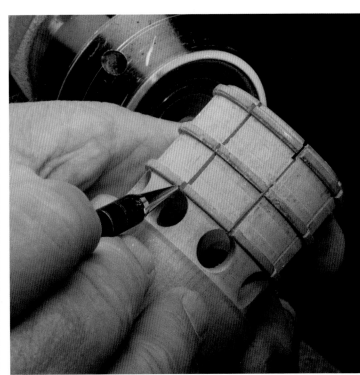

My next step was to reduce the cylinder down in diameter, except for the area being held by the screw chuck. The mean outside diameter is 2". The only variations in diameter are the shoulders, which need only be high enough to trap the hose clamps. In other words, everything is 2" in diameter, including the surface underneath the clamps. When you form the shoulders, keep them uniform in height. I am pointing with the pencil to one of the clamping areas. The clamps were trapped strictly as a convenience, to keep them in alignment so I could tighten them with one hand. You can see from the previous photos there are two clamps. I will explain their functions later. Now comes the fun part.

The next step is to cut the fingers. The hose clamps have been removed here so you can see this better. The vee block with which I drilled the 1/2" holes on the drill press was also used to cut the fingers. The 1/2" hole in the vee block was drilled deep enough to hold a 1/2" dowel, long enough to go through the cylinder. The end of the vee block had to be trimmed to allow the shoulders to set parallel in the vee block. Next, the vee block was taken to the band saw and aligned with the fence to the center of the hole or vee block. I then cut from the end to the 1/2" hole, rotating it four times. In other words, I did nothing more than index the rotation of the chuck on the dowel, which cut the fingers to a uniform width. Upon finishing the cutting, sand the inside corners of the fingers to help prevent marring the egg's surface when you later tighten the clamps.

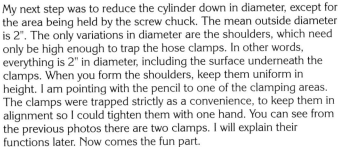

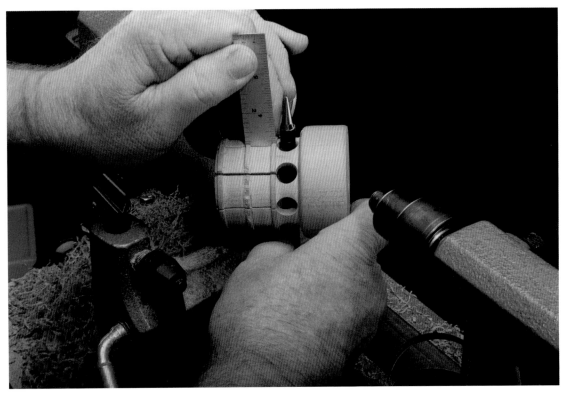

Envision the pencil as being the dowel in the vee block and the scale as the band saw blade. The more care you take making the chuck, the better it will work. This is not a futile exercise. If you make a collection of eggs, you will feel better showing off quality Grade A eggs, rather than just eggs.

All too often when you write a book you think of things that could have been done differently *after* the book has already gone to print. This time I was lucky, as I had this brainstorm (at two in the morning out of a sound sleep) before the final editing . . .

Most people only have a limited availability of 3" *dried* hard maple. After contemplation, I came up with the alternative of using PVC (polyvinyl chloride)—basically speaking, plastic pipe. You can obtain a multitude of sizes with various fittings. By gluing up whatever sizes are necessary to obtain your final fit, the possibilities are limitless. The advantage of the PVC over wood is that there is no grain in the PVC. The main reason we are making this chuck is to center an object. When using wood, if the grain pattern is not equal, the fingers will contract at a different ratio to each other, making a very minute difference to the circumference. In other words, it won't center the object being held. When using PVC pipe, however, there is no grain to contend with. In other words, all the fingers expand or contract at an equal ratio. With the uniformity of the PVC fingers, you stand a much better chance of holding the egg or object you are working on much more concentrically. Another good feature is that with various fittings, cleaner, and glue, the possibilities for holding with this type of chuck are again limitless. To make the chuck shown here, I used a 1-1/2" coupling and a short section of pipe to give the egg end sufficient material to hold it. The basic measurements carry over from the previously made wooden egg chuck. The size of the chuck end would be composed of whatever size is necessary to match your chuck. The end result will be an external or internal hold to suit your situation, depending on the chuck used.

We have at this time explored the possibilities of an egg or finger chuck, yet there are so many other possibilities for using this type of application. I often wonder how many more are out there. Necessity is again the mother of invention. Keep on inventing.

The reason we did not cut the ends off the egg is twofold. First, we did not want to chance tearing end grain and leaving a hole. Second, we are going to use the end to set the egg up concentric in the chuck.

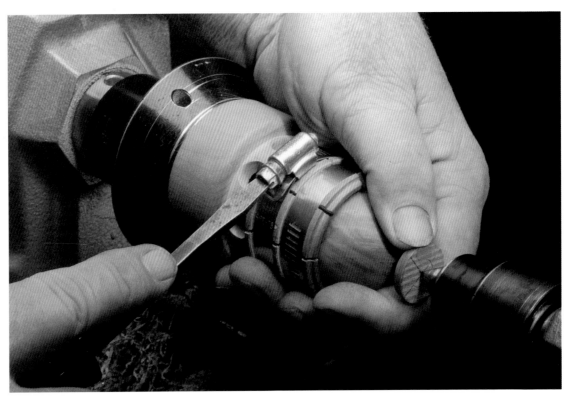

Put the 60° point into the existing drive hole on the end of the egg and push the egg against the point while tightening the rear clamp lightly. I tighten the rear clamp first as it forces the fingers together more uniformly. The front clamp helps to hold the egg securely.

Now tighten the front clamp snugly, making sure that it's positioned 180° from the other. That will help tighten more uniformly. Over-tightening either clamp could dent your egg, depending on the wood used. This sequence should line the egg up so we can turn the end. If the egg is slightly out of concentricity, we will still be able to blend our finished surfaces together. The farther the fingers have to travel, the less accurate the chuck will be. That is one of the reasons I try to set a uniform diameter. Now given Murphy's Law, you know that fantastic piece of wood you just found for your egg collection won't clean up to that desired diameter. A fix will be to wrap masking tape around the smaller egg after turning, in order to increase its diameter before placing in the chuck. It may not run perfectly true, but then eggs are not perfectly uniform either.

Take a parting tool and cut off most of the excess wood.

Before turning on the lathe, always rotate it by hand to make sure everything clears. Here is a prime example where the clamp could be on the back side and you would move the tool rest too close without realizing it. It can happen. Also, make sure your tool rest and support are locked down so they do not move during use. This is how I destroyed the chuck I mentioned previously.

Leave a nubbin so you can cut the end of the egg cleanly, avoiding any tear out.

Shape the end of the egg.

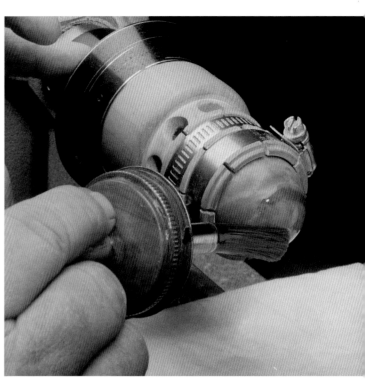

Apply finish as normal, then turn on the lathe and buff. Again, when you are buffing, remember those hose clamps swinging around.

Sand, then check the end of the egg to make sure you have no concentric marks or burnished areas as we want the end to be uniform with the rest of the egg.

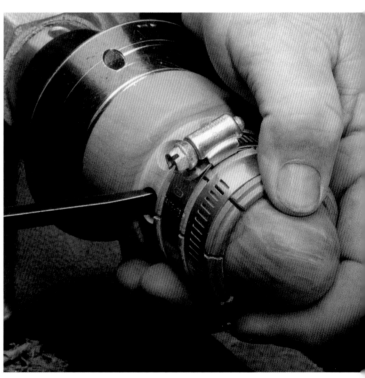

Loosen your clamps and remove the egg from the chuck. Sometimes, when trying to pull the egg out of the chuck, its shape makes your fingers tend to push it back rather than pull it out. See how those holes come into play?

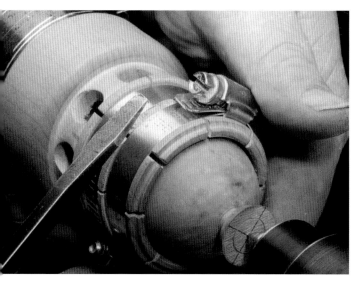

Reverse the egg and install as before. It does not matter whether you start with the front or back – this is basically the same as which came first, the chicken or the egg.

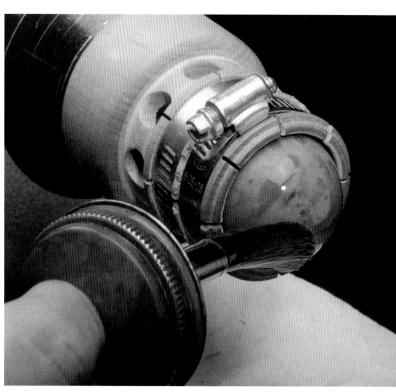

Apply finish as normal. I normally use a loose bound buffing wheel and wax after my finish of Deft™ has dried. This gives the egg a great look and feel.

Cut off the excess as before and shape the end of the egg.

The egg is completed.

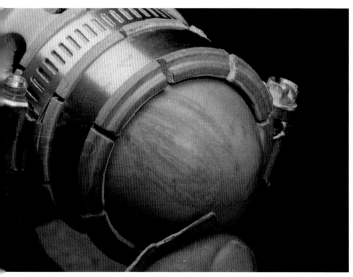

Sand the egg, blending together the surfaces.

Kaleidoscope Eggs

As long as we are into eggs, let's make another variation—a kaleidoscope egg. There are various kaleidoscope kits available from different suppliers that are suitable for eggs. Instructions are included, covering all phases from blank size to assembly. Normally, these are made on a mandrel with corresponding bushings. If you are planning to make several, this is definitely the way to go. Occasionally, you may want to try one kit, whether it be a kaleidoscope egg or some other type of mandrel/bushing setup. Rather than purchasing the necessary mandrel and bushings and ending up dissatisfied with the results obtained (as well as with a mandrel and set of bushings you may never use again), we will make our own setup. This setup is not necessarily just for kit projects, but is a great way to learn a different method that is applicable to various turning situations.

I am starting with a block of kingwood, approximately 2" x 2" x 2-5/16", held in a four jaw chuck.

Our particular kit calls for a 13/16" hole to be drilled through the block.

TIP: I have yet to find a wood lathe that did not have a slight amount of play in the tailstock. If the tailstock is locked down in its most out of line position, the result will be an oversized hole. What I prefer to do, is leave the tailstock loose, start the lathe, and lightly bring up the tailstock until the point of the drill is lightly touching the work piece. The rotation of the work piece against the drill point will self center the tailstock to the best possible alignment of the lathe. If your lathe is way out of alignment, this may help but it will not be a cure-all. At this point, lock down the tailstock, then continue to drill. I use the same concept when doing spindle work, if possible.

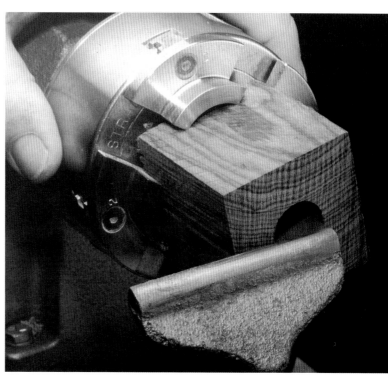

The hole has been drilled and I am now cleaning and squaring up the end.

Take out the block and reverse it in the chuck, making sure that your cleaned up surface is flat against the jaws. This is so the work piece and hole stay in alignment.

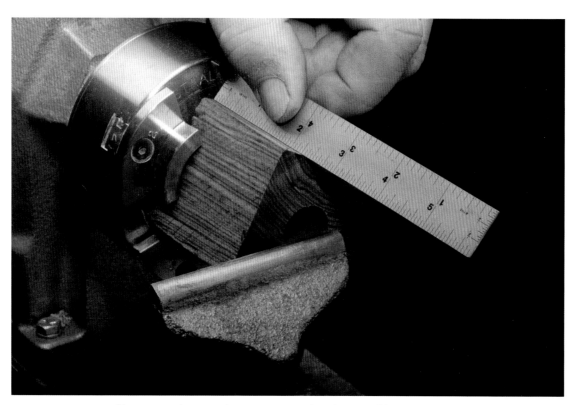

Clean up and square the remaining end so the overall length is 2-1/4" (our kit dimension). Then remove the block from the chuck.

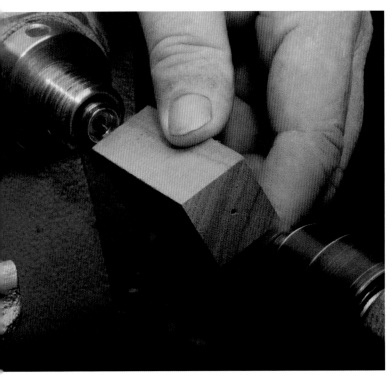

We are now going to create a mandrel and bushings. I have a cone dead center in the headstock and a cone live center in the tailstock. I also have a piece of scrap hardwood, 1" square by 3-1/4". Mark the centers of the blank and put in the lathe.

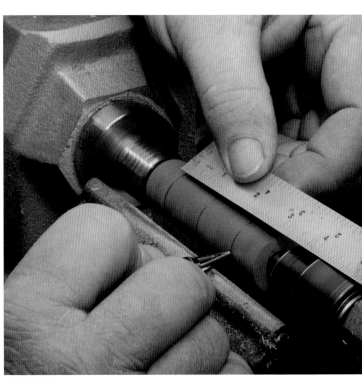

Mark out the center of the work piece and 1" on either side of the center.

Clean up the piece to a cylinder.

With a parting tool, slightly mark off your ends.

With a skew, turn and size the center section to 13/16". Use care doing this as it is going to have to go inside the hole in the egg blank, which will support and drive it.

Reducing down to our required diameter.

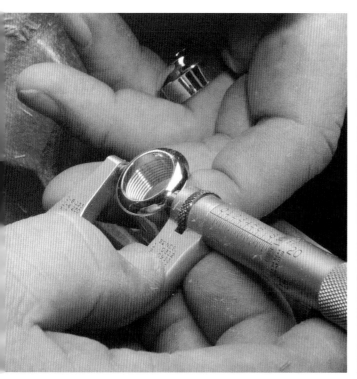

Take the two end caps from the kaleidoscope kit and measure them, as we are going to make the ends of this mandrel match those dimensions. I am using a micrometer, which I believe is the best way to measure a round object. In addition, I carried one for years in my previous occupation. It's like an old friend.

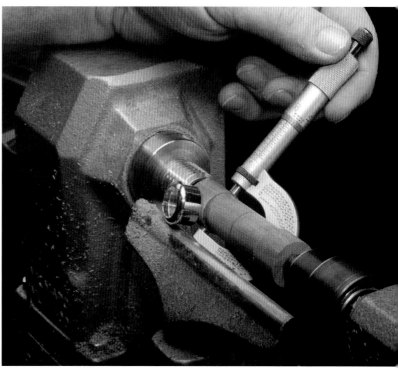

This shoulder is now the same diameter as the metal end piece.

The other shoulder has been completed as well.

Using a parting tool, cut the piece in half.

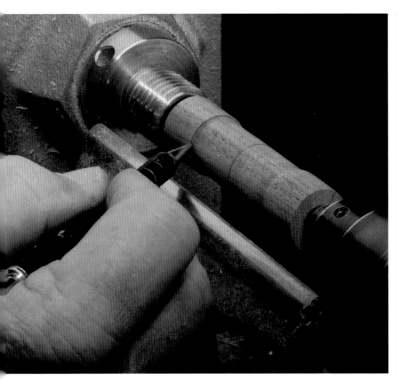

Make sure the shoulders on both ends are clean and sharp as these will be tight against our work piece.

Take the two halves and put them in their respective ends of the egg blank. Since the blank is 2-1/4" long and we have a little less 2" of mandrel, there is a gap between them where the two halves do not touch. This is important. If for some reason the dimensions of the mandrel were altered and the two pieces did touch inside the egg, the dimensioned shoulders would not contact, support, and drive the blank.

Starting to shape the egg.

Developing the shape.

Using the caliper and a parting tool, I am setting the diameter that I want for my egg.

More shaping. Pay attention to the bushings on each end, as the egg's final dimension must match these. Our goal is to have the egg's curve or form blend with the end caps.

Getting close to our finished size. Once we reach that, we will sand.

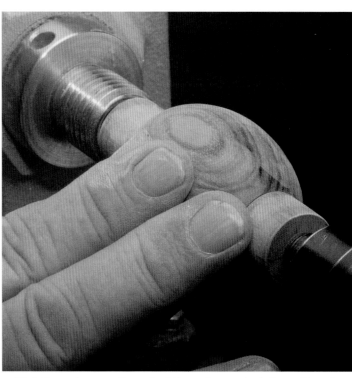

Work through your grits and, at the end, stop the lathe and hand sand with the grain to eliminate your concentric marks.

Sanding the egg.

Apply the finish of your choice. I'm using Deft™ again.

Remove the finished egg from the lathe and pull the two plugs from the ends.

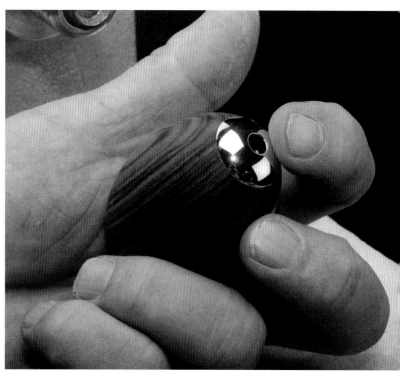

Try the metal parts and make sure you are satisfied with the fit. If the match between the egg and end caps is not to your liking, you can assemble the plugs and egg in the lathe again and make adjustments.

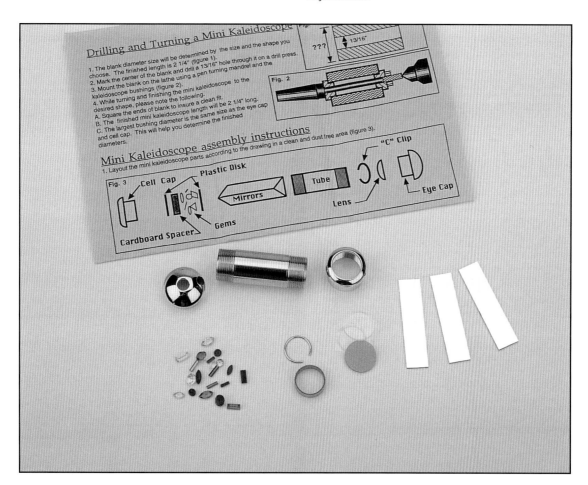

The layout of the parts in the kaleidoscope kit before assembly.

I've now assembled the kit, per the instructions. This is the heart of the kaleidoscope that will go inside the egg.

Remove the eye piece and insert the assembly into the egg.

Screw the eye piece back on the top and your kaleidoscope egg is complete. If everything fits to your satisfaction, remove the kaleidoscope parts and buff the egg with a little wax, then reassemble. I have found through experience that to get a quality image you need to keep *everything* clean. I also believe it's a misconception that all of the beads supplied have to be put into the cell cap. If all the beads are used, it becomes too crowded and your images cannot be formed easily. In other words, the beads must be able to move freely. When choosing the beads to use, pick the colors you like. You can also add other objects, such as seeds, etc. Throughout the process, think, rather than just following the instructions.

The Finish Jar

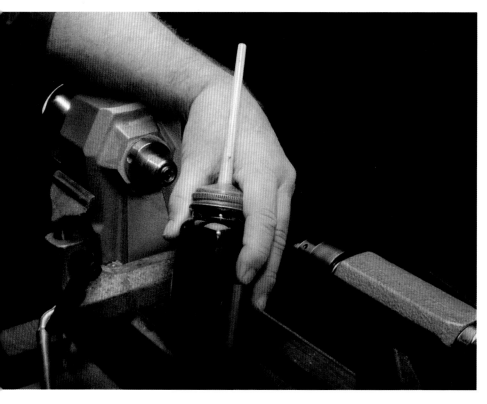

This is my finish jar. As I use this jar, I am often asked what the finish is, to which I respond "It's a secret, that's why I keep it in a brown bottle." Actually it's Deft™. This finish jar has been in my previous books and I have received numerous phone calls from around the country asking where I purchased it. Naturally, I made this jar. As with any other project, you never think of all the possibilities when you make your first one. To create it, I reinforced the lid on the outside with a piece of wood epoxied to the top of the lid, drilled a hole in the center (completely through the lid), then inserted my brush and epoxied it in place. After it was dry, I put my favorite finish (Deft™) into the jar. Now I could open my jar, apply my finish, and return my brush to the jar without having to clean the brush daily. This worked like a charm. One day, however, my brush came loose from the lid. Failing to think about the composition of Deft™ (which is lacquer based), I had not realized the fumes would deteriorate the epoxy over time. After having become accustomed to using my jar, I was not about to lose it without a fight . . .

. . so I cleaned everything up and started over. I used the same procedures in assembling the jar, but after the epoxy had cured, I took the inside of the lid and completely coated the area around the brush with silicone adhesive. This has solved my problem, as it protects the epoxy from the fumes. Perseverance prevails again!

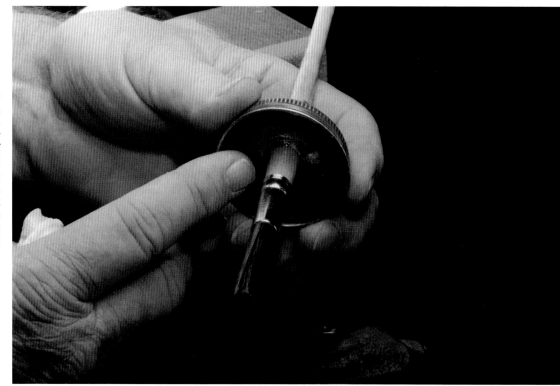

How I Sign My Work

People often look at my signature on my turnings and ask how I do it. Number one, I happen to be blessed with legible writing. This makes it easier. I use a wood burning pen and will be happy to walk you through the procedure that I use. There are various techniques learned through experience over the years. Pay attention as this is hot off the pen.

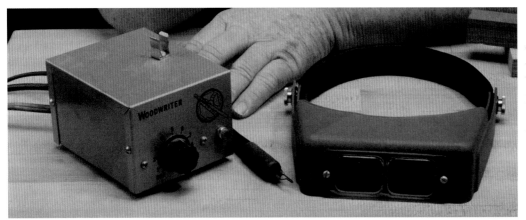

The equipment that I use is simply a woodburning unit with a rheostat that will allow variable temperature settings. The pen itself is a signature tip which has been modified. And, even if you have good vision, some type of magnification is needed.

Here is a side view of the pen's tip.

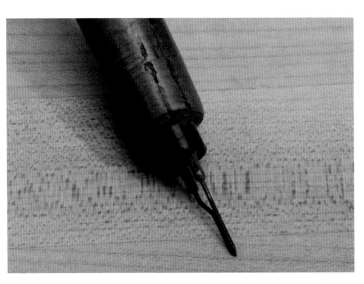

And here is a top view. To start with, I took a smooth, 6" mill file and worked the point close to what it is now. I made it much more pointed, with less material, than its standard design. When I got close to my desired shape, I took a fine stone and refined the point even more, until it reached its present state. The point should be smooth, with no facets, so it sort of glides on the writing surface. As you can see, there isn't a lot of material holding the top and bottom wires together. If you turned the heat up as high as it would go, I'm sure it would melt the tip. Oops. . . Instead, I treat the tip as fragile, using a lower heat and working my way up, rather than starting too hot and working my way down. Using it this way has not given me any problems, and this particular tip is at least twelve years old. I do have a backup. If I didn't, I'm sure I would have burned out the original one years ago – Murphy's Law again. If you modify your tip as such and use it with care, yours should last a reasonable length of time as well.

I always told myself my vision was good, and it is. But when trying to sign my name and some information on wood, I realized, as I improved, that I had to see – really see – what I was doing. To do this I use a magnifying visor. Any kind of magnification, such as a magnifying light or anything else you do not have to hold in your hand, would be adequate.

Wood itself is the largest variable in writing on wood. The finer the grain and the harder the texture, the better the writing. A piece of hard maple with its uniform grain and hard texture allows you to write on it beautifully. Conversely, a piece of white oak with its coarse grain, large pores, and distinction between winter growth and summer growth presents problems. Looking down on the growth rings on a tree, you can see each year's growth—under close scrutiny, you can distinguish the winter growth from the summer growth. The summer growth comprises the majority of the annual ring because of its growth through the end of spring, summer, and the beginning of fall. Because this larger area was produced relatively fast, it is softer than the winter growth. During the winter, when the tree becomes dormant and the sap retreats, the tree is still growing. Under the adverse conditions of winter the growth is very minute and much harder.

As you can see, this disc of hard maple accepts writing very easily.

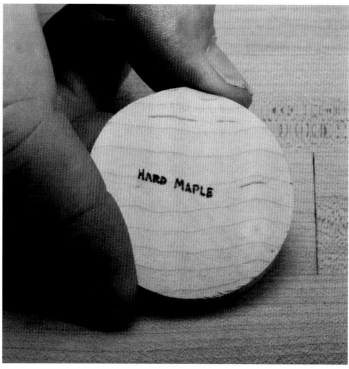

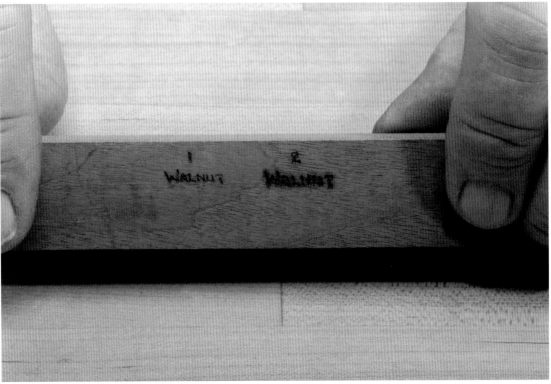

Walnut can be good or can be bad, depending on the coarseness of the grain. On this piece, the writing labeled (1) is totally different than the writing labeled (2). Number 2 had the heat turned up too high and I was pressing too hard.

Here are a few illustrations on oak. The first one, labeled (1), is how I would normally sign oak. I find it quite legible. The second, labeled (2), has the heat turned up, probably a little too high. The third, labeled (3), has the heat turned down but I was pressing against the wood too hard. What does this mean? The real secret to writing on wood is not to burn into the wood, but to write *on* the surface. This is where the magnification enters into the picture. You have to be able to see that you are gently writing on the wood, and that the heat—not the pressure—is burning the wood. When you press too hard, the pen follows the variation between the winter growth and the summer growth and creates a situation just as if it were going down a washboard. This results in very little darkness on the winter growth and a deep black area on the summer growth – or very non uniform writing. Additionally, my signature and information is written very small. Not because I am ashamed of my work, but because I would rather not take away from it. Here again, the fine tip and being able to see with the magnification is a definite help.

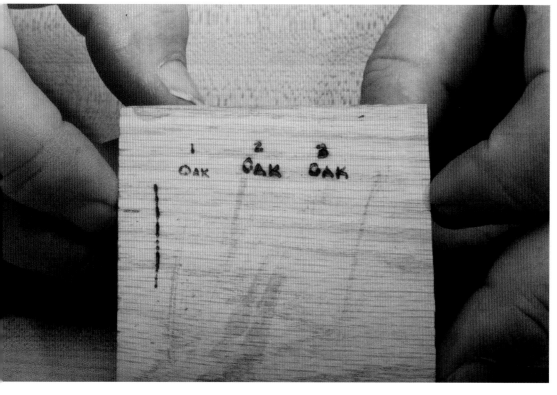

Before signing one of your treasures, take a piece of scrap, preferably the same wood as your project, and practice. Don't practice on a fresh sawn cut, use a scrap that has been surfaced so that it replicates the actual surface of your project. Normally, you sign your work after your project has had finish applied to it. The finish will burn or flash up around the burned area. When you have completed the signing, therefore, take some 0000 steel wool and lightly scrub the surface of the burned area. This will clean up those flashings and leave much more legible writing. Then hit it with a little of your finish. I'm sure I have missed something and will probably think of it after this book has been published. But as of now, this is Dick Sing—signing off.

The Gallery

I have always enjoyed watching the patterns that clouds make and seeing images in them. I was very excited when Dick gave me an Easter egg that actually had the Easter bunny in it. Also, in 1999, before we went to Australia, Dick turned an ornament that went straight into our collection as it had the continent of Australia on it. Can you see what I see in the next few pages?

—Cindy Sing

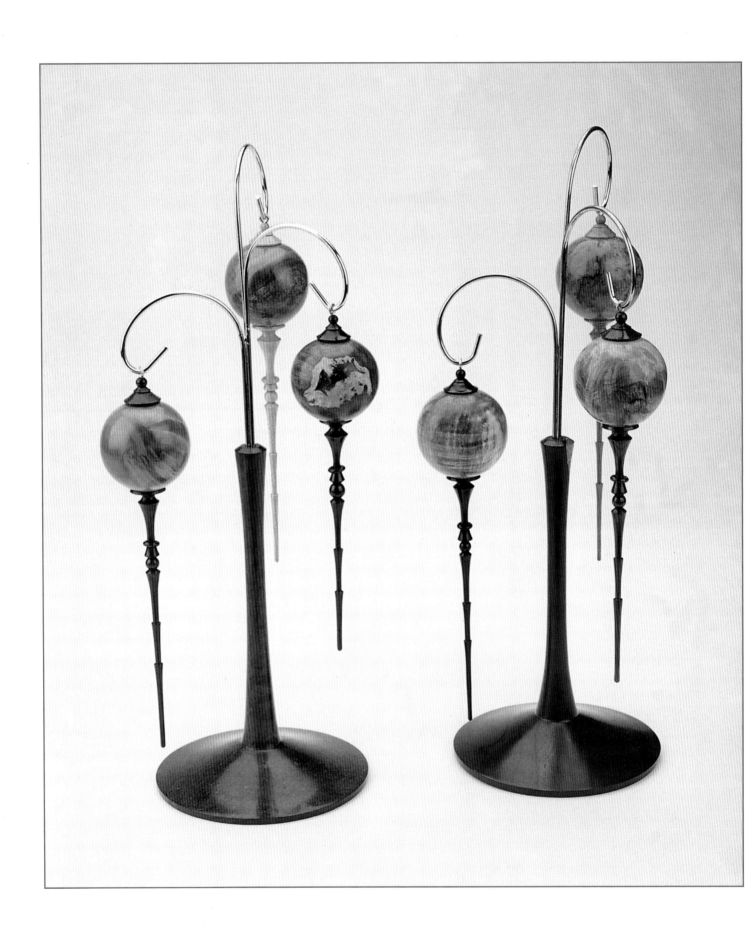

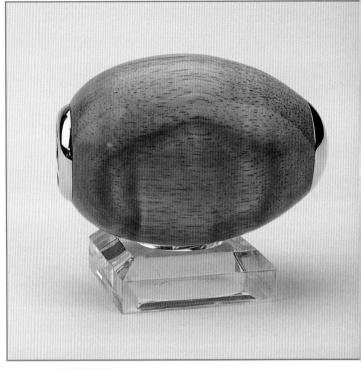

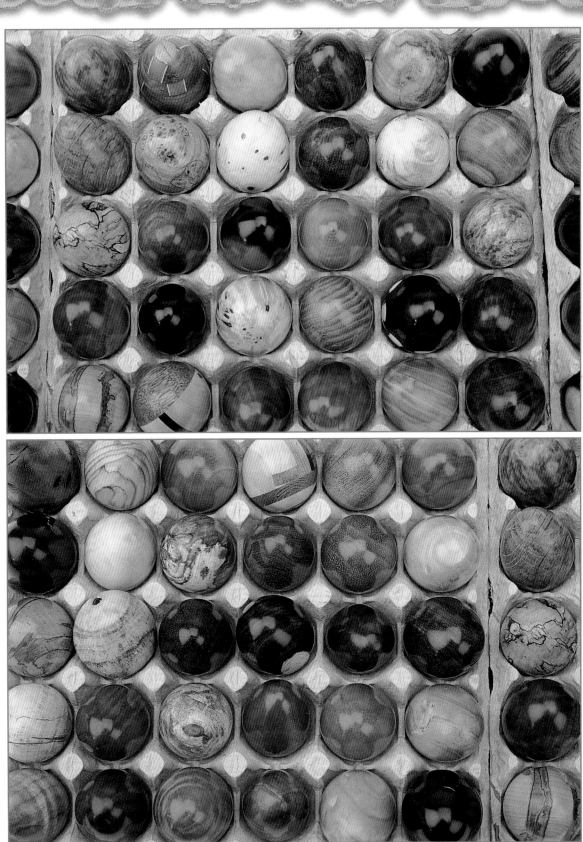